LENS

POETRY OF ART IN CALIFORNIA

Grace Marie Grafton

LENS

POETRY OF ART IN CALIFORNIA

For Rich, with my best wishes
Grace Marie Grafton

Grace Marie Grafton

LENS
Copyright©2019 Grace Marie Grafton
All Rights Reserved
Published by Unsolicited Press
Printed in the United States of America.
First Edition 2019.

AUTHOR'S NOTE:
The poems in **LENS** are written to paintings from the books: *California Art, 450 Years of Painting and Other Media*, published by Dustin Publications, Los Angeles 1998 and *Room to Breathe, The Wild Heart* of the San Francisco Peninsula, published by Heyday Books 2012, coupled with the author's extensive knowledge of the history and environment of California. Below each poem is the name of the artist and the title of the painting that inspired the poem.

Attention schools and businesses: for discounted copies on large orders, please contact the publisher directly. Books are brought to the trade by Ingram.

For information contact:
Unsolicited Press
Portland, Oregon
www.unsolicitedpress.com
orders@unsolicitedpress.com
619-354-8005

Cover Design: Kathryn Gerhardt
Editor: Nathan Burgess
Cover Art: The Wave by Arthur Matthews
ISBN: 978-1-950730-05-6

Table of Contents

AWE

High Sierra, 1878

Where they got off the horses,
almost rusted to the saddle,
how many more days with
the high peaks, white drama,
still before them? The incredible
light a gewgaw they tossed
between them, altitude skewing
thought, changing their words into
bubbles and baubles. But —
creaky joints set down alongside
creeks so new they dashed and
washed the rocks, wet the air,
swooped — clattered — roared.
No stopping the water, wasn't
that what they came for? Climbing
on those horses, abandoning
good sense to ride four, five
days into this feral, unleashed
land available only in summer
and here they were, subject to
its unreasonable solutions.

"Kings River Canyon"
William Keith, 1878

The Beach

These people who gravitate to water,
the beach, the blank sky, clouded sky, storm
speaking the well-known, threatening song.
Picnic baskets wrestled through sand,
young mother under a rigged-up tent.
Nursing her infant, introducing him to
the waves' beat and shush-shush
on the shore. Father in bare feet —
the way clear surf curls around skin,
a friendly hand, lyric phrase.
Before the gray rain, before the whale's
washed-up corpse, before the flies or
sand fleas. Pay the price. Sunburn,
grit under bathing suit's band.
A sense of escape worth the bother,
the memory of many someones
who launched into this strange,
familiar element, laid out on their backs,
nothing blocking their gaze. Let the swells
lift and lower them while underneath
whisper the bones, the life inside shells,
spikes, scales, fins, hunger, the Other.

"Santa Monica"
Ernest Narjot, 1889

The Artist Paints the Light

The light in Yosemite Valley lifts his mind
to the height of granite cliffs and
there he is, next to a black oak,
trunk a solid soldier ready to ascend
with him into the impossible ether.
His vision rises to the topmost leaves,
shares the compulsion
to merge with unadulterated light,
how it rushes out of blue and white
to slather them into the actuality
it will become. He understands that,
even though light, to those static, seems
the most desirable existence,
light itself longs to be leaf, petal,
lash and eye that sees.

"Looking Up the Yosemite Valley"
Albert Bierstadt, 1863

Burning in San Francisco Bay

The fiery ship in the bay
could remind a man of the sought-after
gold. Gold which brought many
here. Gold that might have,
at the moment of conflagration,
been in the ship's hold. And the many
skiffs, each carrying one man
trying to get close enough to board and grab,
despite the danger, despite the punishing odds.
Mesmerizing, this color, this molten adventure,
enough to turn him into a fool. Does he
love the gold? Melting into the water.
The loss, the sorrow, after visions of
great fortune.

"Fire in San Francisco Bay, July 24, 1853"
Charles Christian Nahl, 1856

Hunter

Mountain lion and man, sleek beauties,
one born in enviable fur, the other
donning deftly-woven wool coat
and trousers. The man's soft black
scarf echoes healthy black hair,
sets in relief his white shirt.
Laundered and pressed by
someone who perhaps came near
swooning over his handsome face.
Strength and determination
still seem almost alive
in the tawny form stretched
at his feet, paws and toothy snout
displayed. Man and cat, bodies
of equal weight. Only one had a gun.

"Peter Quivey and the Mountain Lion"
Charles Christian Nahl, 1857

Rocks

It was the end of the world for those
who wished to go farther west.
Anyone with a lick of sense knew
you don't go farther than the furrowed
rocks that block the beach.
Those rocks surf attacked, cracked,
delineated age undenied, yet not
shown proudly, like some old
sea captain's, each line boasting
another battle against nature
won. This promontory a craggy
foot, no dialogue here.
Setting sun casts red color to a dun
hump of stolid strength, to the white
ruffled foam kinder waves string
along the beach's path, leading
a walker face to face with
what a human cannot change.
Only an equal, only unaccountable time,
unintended patience, unmeant surrender.

"Golden Gate"
Raymond Dabb Yelland, 1882

Chef of the Palace Hotel

A man who cooks for others
rolls up his sleeves
     ah, these sleeves on this white coat
     this coat with its double row
     of buttons, with its tea-rose boutonniere
     slightly wrinkled, just as
his mouth slightly smiles, his eyes
a bit soft in their 'does this please you?'
expression. He's a sculptor
of the culinary arts and holds
his offering in his hands.
     His hands
     a platter holding a platter
     holding an array,
     a décor, a masterpiece
that will be eaten.
What every artist truly wants:
that his art be consumed.

"Jules Harder, First Chef of the Palace Hotel"
Joseph Harrington, 1874

Easter Harvest

The calla lilies' white tongues lap the moonlight
over and over until the field they fill becomes
a blanket of light he could lie on under
the moon-washed sky. A star here and there.
Orion and the lilies of April, moving him
out of life's shortness into beauty's longevity.
The barn is far and quiet. Cows don't mow
this field. He's found a way to make
beauty pay. Counting on the human hunger
for forgiveness, for the way lilies bring to mind
angels' wings or the vanilla custard Grandmother
made specially for Brother and him before
he had to worry about whether to plant
flowers or alfalfa, or how to get enough water
to the ditches. About river access, about
permission to cross the neighbor's property.
But now, these lilies, and energy enough
to be out ten o'clock at night not for irrigation
but for gifts.

"An Easter Offering"
Charles Walter Stetson, 1896

Failed Story

White roses on the bier of the legendary
princess, mythical maiden dead
in the grip of her beauty. Fond wish,
brocaded robe, the white petals soon to
break and drift on waters the dark stranger
ferries her over. Her adorned remains,
we should say, not *her*. All that we
mourn, the unrealized. Dark
faceless stranger, plain in black
robes. The man of business, who
does what's necessary so that, through
our lives, we can weep and remember
the waters that swallowed our shining
intentions, the words that failed
to lure the coins to our coffers,
the helplessness we repeatedly felt
when we couldn't grasp the reasons
we didn't win the war or get to board
the train or heal the wound or talk to God.

"Elaine"
Toby Rosenthal, 1874

River under Redwoods

Here it's evening, no house to tuck into,
hide away from mountain lion or rattler.
Day-birds have flown their last chittering
trip to roost in dimming madrones, oaks,
and bays that crowd the creek corridor.
The camper plans to stay, though he
chooses not to lie under the giant reach
of the redwoods. He's been told
that these trees house spirits.
He doesn't know if he believes in 'spirits,'
but these trees that render everything to
shade and silence, even in the daytime,
arouse awe and bewilderment in him.
So he thinks he won't take a chance.
Build his fire on the flat near the stream,
rig up the sticks for his tarp, listen
for the owls to start their hunt.

"Twilight Scene with Stream and Redwood Trees"
Julian Rix, 1900

LAND'S END

Coming into . . .

The canyon for the first time, the brown
hill to the south with its gold undercolor
like nothing her old life could offer. She felt
uncertain, then, of what she wanted or could
love. Of how to depart from forest and water
she knew she could count on. Kaleidoscopic green,
turn as she might, leaves, vines, undergrowth
with required mistiness in every degree. Here,
the hills, even the ground squirrels, stark, ragged.
Flora, air so naked she can see the dry grass
blades distinct from each other a mile away.
Hawk vision. Hawk heart rising into what
seems so simple. No untangle required.

"Mountain"
Francis McComes, 1908

Canyon, Santa Barbara

This canyon, before it turned into town.
Picture the same stone over and over,
white, slightly rounded, unencumbered by
the conviction that people and their shelters
deserve attention's spotlight. In nineteen-
oh-two, only one red-tiled roof, only
a single tower among the no-holds-barred
fescue that claimed the winter slopes. And
the live-oak trees never bare of black-green
leaves and the black squirrels like swatches
of laughter in the limbs. Unimpeded rivulets
and water courses during rain's season.
Convocation of acorns, squalling jays,
the absence of car wheels or horns or lights
or streets. Room for moon's silence.

"In Mission Canyon, Santa Barbara"
Henry Joseph Breuer, 1902

Come True

Down in the canyon, sunset clouds
a shawl of promise, needles of the twisted
spruce winnow surrendered sun into air.
Autumn sky, ground cover singed
toward rusted flame, the sycamore
far downslope in the watershed granting
the painter's preference for renderable
hues. Just as cooling air begins
to nip fingertips, nose sniffs clarifying
sage, mesquite. The rock she sits on.
A life, finally, where she can hike
and feel herself swell with a pleasure
tonally akin to that swelling cloud
as it drifts away from hilltops
just visible.

"San Gabriel Canyon"
Marion Kavanaugh Wachtel, 1915

Houseboats

Those who love to live on water. Not in but
stilted above the lap, lap that sucks against
pilings. The scent. Skin guaranteed moist,
moon raying reflection across liquid night.
Look out the window, it's always moving.
This wood they live in, semi-permanent, with
change all around it. So the mind floats,
unstuck, unfixed, unfurled. The occasional
glass of whiskey, evening murmur, early mist,
noon dapple. Ever sliding down the slide.

"Arks along Lagoon"
Seldon Connor Gile, 1926

Land's End

Building near the ocean's edge,
weren't they afraid? Pacific a misnomer,
those waves can be past hungry.
In storms, moon's pull woos water
over the beach, through doorways,
rushes into a monstrous moaning.
Any observer foolish enough to be
out on the headlands in such a storm
hopes there's a back door somewhere,
hopes they've all gone to town. Or that
they long ago realized the blue and white,
the shush-shush beat, the innocent yellow
days when everything seems possible
in the clarity of the air, weren't worth
enduring the sudden surges and fear.
So they abandoned the place. Gave up
what she called 'the beat of God's heart,'
moved into town, promised each other
they'd bicycle out at least once a week,
stay over in their once-upon-a-time
concrete hideaway, wade in the waves,
build, again, castles in the sand.

"Shoreline"
Guy Rose, 1920

What the Wave Gives

If we start at the bottom
      (how deep did she dive?)
near the coast, we will find
      (a fish, a mermaid?)
white shells and the octopus
      (woman, flashing skin?)
like a bulbous shell itself, winding
      (wavery catching sun's colors)
in and out of the shell-shelf
      (within bubbles streaming)
under water's shift and heave
      (off her skin, out her hair)
guide for human curiosity, path
      (lifting arms, her flesh, her wish)
in and out of the undergird
      (propelling red as though were blood)
into air so we can see
      (the unexplained that waters keep)

"The Wave (Marine)"
Arthur Matthews, 1915

Alone

She lives away from others,
under three white-barked aspen
whose leaves turn orange in October,
bringing in the notion of fire
that gets a person through the January chill.
Just now, out her kitchen window,
tree aflame, she can't imagine a lesser
light, can't call up the feeling
of frost. But it will come, and
the skeletal limbs will look gnarled,
sketched in against a sky
of rare rain. Creek bed dry
through most of the year. How do
the frogs survive? But out pop their
trills and burps as soon as the drops
lash down, darkening the evergreens'
trunks. White aspen bark remains
white, gleams silver in the unkind rain,
more bony and helpless as though
there had never been orange fire
that swathed its body.

"Hermitage"
William Wendt, 1919

Homestead

He continues to tell his story, though
he doesn't think of it that way.
Coming to feel this place as home. To love
the way the wild oats and sticky monkey flower
turn gold and brown by June and
there's no rain from May first
deep into September. No rain, yet
fog whispers over this night or that,
lingers as morning mist. In the sandy-
colored shirt she sewed him, he goes
to the hen house to collect eggs.
Barn owls call their basso notes.
He can smell the skunk has
made its weekly inspection, hoping for
a careless mistake. He's not careless any-
more. After gathering three or four eggs,
he'll pull her out of the kitchen, they'll
pick the plums off the tree they planted
eight years ago and boil them into jam.
She'll hold out the spoon to him,
invite him with her eyes as he licks.

"Sonoma County, Landscape"
Jules Page, 1920

Thirst

These trees are so sparse, just
skinny sticks really. The horses
that visit the river to drink and
bathe each day rub against the unresisting
bark, wear it thinner, thinner until
even with roots so near water
the trees' life force must feel squeezed,
in danger of exposure. Bleed sap
through a crack. And the horses
can't be blamed, it's dry country.
They need the shade, need to feel
something cool and lithe and
non-animal on their hairy hides.
As though caring lips whispered to them,
'I'll scratch your back, I'll understand
your need for water, I'll be a thing
to touch your rump.' Some things
live together in the dry hills, stay
near the gift-river that can give
no explanation for its presence in this
leached land.

"By the River"
Clayton S. Price, 1927

Noon   or: Southwest

Heat, and its relationship with rocks,
its unremitting spectrum. Yellow-red
changes the blue of a stranger's eyes.
Wait for night, sage advice, but then
I couldn't see what a rock's face
might impart. Even at midnight, heat
radiates onto a hand held against
the rough plane. Get tough,
the desert landscape teaches.
I've learned, my skin is not
like the rock's, though rocks
peel too. A decade at a time,
scraping here and there, a crack
breathes a little trickle of air,
especially in mid-December
when the sky has broken loose
from Sun's strict dominion and
the stranger enters, Stranger Snow,
searching for a rare rapprochement.

"Jawbone Canyon"
Conrad Buff, 1925

Lone Pine and Mt. Whitney

The mountains and their lunatic height provide
so ready a drama the settlers need never fear
going soft, being bored, or feeling life is too
easy. Almost perpendicular, the peaks rise
behind the desert house and corral. Early sun
smacks an implacable presence right into
their waking. They look up to see lines of snow
in the high crevices all summer long while
their lowland creek relinquishes May girth to
a couple inches of ripple. The house-garden gasps,
cottonwood trees and creosote bushes seem
to cough in the drying wind and there's no way
to cool the kitchen down. Up there the stark peaks,
granite gray, perfectly match snow's
white vocabulary. It seems they hear it
all the time, something about being so small,
something about being snarled up in the
minute to minute rumple of meals and
laundry and pumping water for baths.
Look, the cliffs seem to say, look at what it means
to be relinquished into what's beyond breath,
beyond fingernails or food or how to
make yourself understood.

"Near Lone Pine, California"
John Frost, 1924

Bargain

The most beautiful glitter, fairytale moon,
shine sifted, lifted, churned into polished frost
by light-footed surf. 'No containment,'
we think, but even the ocean must be contained
within its bowl. Go beneath, see through
glass goggles, the neon tetra flash,
follow blue-and-green parrot fish, scales
gold. Swept away in beauty's bargain,
heart rises as wave swells, sun
scatters color, blood vessels jig.
The long-sought family, rock-sisters,
sand-dune mothers, Grandma Sky
in her purple hems, brother tern
teaching us to fly and wheel and return.

"Moon Path across the Sea"
William Ritschel, 1924

Friends

Muriel, the day she wore her green dress
with the white collar and cuffs, loved
that particular green with a touch of blue
in the creases, reminded her (reminded
the whole bridge club) of Kentucky 'blue grass,'
though none of us West Coast girls had been
there. Still, the fabric held water, didn't it,
in the sense that ponds or lawns seem to
float? We don't have much of that new-grass
hue in Southern California. And she would
wear a hat, not a straw hat either. Covered
the red in her hair, she must've meant to
cover the gray. I never noticed the gray,
she was always an 'auburn-haired beauty'
to me, dear soul with her amber beads,
matching so perfectly the dry hills around here.
Though, from far enough away, the hills look
blue, afford the eyes a little relief, like her dress,
like her hat that made us think of winter.
Though winter is fairly warm here, there are
a few days in January when we wake
to frost on the hibiscus we planted in the yard
and think, "I wonder if it will kill it?"

"Muriel"
Annie Baldaugh, 1925

34

EARTH BOUND

The Central Valley

Late afternoon, sunslant pulling
the hard light out of the trees, mixing
leaves into some kind of forgiveness
when there's not a lot more she can
do although the cow needs milking
and hay, laundry still to be taken
off the line but at seven p.m. the air-infused
cloth will have lost its scorch-smell and
remind her of this morning's water
in sheets she pressed against her skin
as she clipped them up. The even ground
of the pasture in shadow invites her
now that the sky's glare has eased.
Thunderheads pile over the mountains,
air and clouds glow. She feels like
Sunday when church gives her room
to leave her hands idle in her lap,
listen to the shuffle and creak,
breath and coughs of folks around her,
and not have to meet anyone's eyes or ask,
'What can I get you?'

"California"
George Innes, 1894

Salmon Fishing

Pay attention, it's not yesterday
when the bills came due or tomorrow
when the baby steals your wife's looks
away. Waiting in this rolling boat for
the fish to strike. The sea both feeds
and eats you. Eats you if you fail to
mind motor and swells, keep poles and
lines from propeller blades, remember
how a snagged salmon pulls and pulls
to be free. You've heard of the bow going
toward the water, other fishers praying
the waves don't rise and the line don't snap.
Even yank a knife out, cut the line
in two. Some fish are past catching.
Some weather you just don't venture out.
There has to be a bargain struck with
the deep if you want to keep on eating
and not be et.

"Salmon Trawlers"
Armin Hassan, 1918

Vineyard

Though soundless, it talks, loud and incessant,
through dream and into the moon's feeble
littering of the land. Knowing too much about
one thing so it fills all the corridors and nubs,
days and evenings, scent, texture, shape.
He planted all around the house, acres of
vines, lovingly staked them up. Vines need
something to climb on, smother with tendrils,
leaves, longing. And then the watering. Best
time: evening. Pray for rain, dig trenches,
run pipelines from river to roots. Clear away
weeds, watch the skies in spring when bloom
sets, pray then for no rain, and no rain in August
when yellow ripeness cracks at a single cold
drop. Cracks, drips, rots away everything —
attention, pruning, all the nights away from the
babies and their mother, tramping water courses
after sunset, ensuring that water flows in
the right path, no gopher holes to suck it
down the hill, wasted.

"The Grape Arbor"
Thomas Hunt, 1925

Oranges

Oranges, in five or more senses. In the memory,
late December days, fog winding gray wrappers
around the dark shape of the tree. You hoped
the frost would hold off. Small winter suns
glow out of the dark tree, but pick one and
the sugar's not there, pale flesh, a child still.

These winter children need nine months to grow.
Wax cream blossoms in early May, neroli scent a
swim in warm water, the excitement of castanets.
Early February, break the orange's skin, out of
oily fragrance bursts a July laugh. Uncanny,
such cool fruit offers such heat.

Round dark tree holding balls of light that
fit perfectly in the hand and feed the need for
food. Something to share. Break apart
the slices, one for each family member,
sit together sucking something sweet.

"Oranges and Branches"
Donna Schuster, 1928

Chickens

The whites, the mixed blacks populating
the feathers of the tail. The way chickens
enter the back gate of the garden, jerky necks,
pecking, twitchy heads, mesmerizing eyes,
shivering red comb above the beak. What's
that for? Why so nervous and skittery,
busy puffy noisy? Maybe because they can't
fly, though the rooster aggressively and
impressively beats the air with wings that seem
strong enough to raise him off the ground but
mostly just flap in the faces of his flock of following
hens. His harem, his fan club, his cluckers.
Let them loose among the growing vegetables,
they'll find the bugs that nip away the lovely
buds, they'll fertilize the roots, brush the leaves
   — beans, frothy carrots, papery corn —
in a neighborly way, with a grooming touch.

"White Leghorns"
Anne Bremer, 1915

Artichoke Picker

Careful of your fingers, the thistle thorns prick
and the acrid juice of stems sting cuts.
Strong backs for this work, strong backs,
long sleeves, long pants. Grandma
hands you the hat as you leave.
The picking day might start out cool,
even nippy, but, California, April afternoon
gets hot. Gloves would be good but then
the knife slips, stem's hard to grab.
It's piece-work, gotta move, get
those globes into the bags, drag them
to the scales, get them weighed, get paid.
The more bags, the softer the bed you can
sleep in. That counts when you all day
gotta bend, stoop, carry, pull aside
heavy prickly leaves. You can't eat those
'chokes for lunch like summer tomatoes.
'Chokes need a long boil. With tomatoes,
just take along a chunk of bread,
bring bacon in your lunch tin, slice up
those plump juice-balls, it's like eating
a sweet summer sun.

"Artichoke Pickers"
Henrietta Shore, 1936–37

Walnut Grove

A walnut grove is a leisurely place, easy to
walk over its cleared earth, tamped, damp
from regular flooding that plumps the nuts,
lets the leaves grow to large, oval fans lifting
and falling lazily in the rare summer breeze.
The white bark, what a treat, run a hand along,
tree offers no resistance, it's like a friendly dog,
spreads its branches gladly. Little red barn
to store the harvest once it falls littering bare
ground, round green husks still hugging the nut,
tightly enclosed, in its acrid envelope. If left
to dry, crack, and languish on the soil, the nut will
break its shell and unwind a naked white curl
of matter that searches for a place to live.
But the man under the trees, who has raked
and weeded this patch of land, won't let
the seedling take hold. These nuts are for
the larder, holiday cakes, candies, nutbread,
the grandfather sitting near the winter fire,
humming to himself about coming west as he
cracks the shells now freed from that wild green
husk. Pops a few in his mouth. A different life.

"Walnut Tree"
Barse Miller, 1938

During War

Clouded light, spilled on the pond surface,
turns transparency into gleaming white.
White as innocent as six a.m., quiet as roots.
And the new grasses that rainwater,
collected in the trough, has rendered dark
and lank, green no longer.

For these

few clean moments, the walker can halt
the grotesque images of the war he knows
daily ravages the lives of young people
he taught just three years earlier.

Eucalyptus

branches look like bare arms of young
lithe men and women in playful dance.
Full of life, full of 'see how I can bend
without breaking.' How beautiful skin is
and newly-coined muscle beneath.
They move to use strength and radiance
without bayonet or rifle or any need
to split apart flesh or take another's heart.

"Early Morning"
Giuseppe Cadenasso, 1916

Death at an Early Age

Singing the green song before he died.
He imagined himself a woman, newly
free to stroll at night. Where the light
seems blue around the skin, she breaks
into shattered forms that walk together
near the surf and hear the harmonies
waterdrops have and will ever make.
He did this before he died,
he died before he could grow old,
of what was called the Spanish Flu.
It's believed, by those who knew him,
that after the evening when the air around
him turned blue, he carried within him
the musics of waves and knew what it is
to be a woman shattered into many forms.
So during his flu, as his fever rose and
held him in fire, he asked to be carried
down to water. They say that he sang
next to the waves as he died.

"My Song"
Rex Slinkard, 1916
(died 1918, age 31)

Internment

Outcast. One among many. The Buddhist
priest with their group says, 'Let what comes
come in the front door. Let it pass through
the house and leave by the back door.'
The outcast is not old, so he can afford to let
some things pass, think of himself as
existing the way the desert exists. He can
put up with the desert where wind blows
sand onto his canvas, into his eyes.
There will likely be other decades
that will demand less endurance
than the cliff he paints, less distance
than the moon he watches grow fat
then skinny. Skinny as he is and of
small importance, yet sky holds them both.

"New Moon, Eagle Pass"
Chiura Obata, 1927

Inhabit

Whose footprint was left under the arches
of the mission? Supposed to be the gate
to a spirit that would guide —

> "Oh Father, these natives, like children
> that do not know Your righteousness,
> see how they stumble in dark ignorance.
> I pray for them that they might learn
> the mercy of Your ways through obedience
> and labor and that they might turn away
> from seeing You in bees and clouds
> and vicious foxes — "

Under the arches painted
with the blue of sky, whose sky, whose
Heaven now fallen in ruins? Whose spirits
are left to occupy land lived on
for thousands of years by the Ohlone
and their neighbors? The grizzlies
now gone, elk no longer found here.
Is this footprint left by the fox who
lives here still, stepping out
into the open darkness now the
Christian brothers are gone and
will not try to trap it?

"Evening Star, Mission Capistrano"
Sydney Laurence, 1935

The Camp

Someone in the camp had been a builder.
> It wasn't really a 'camp.'
> Someday he'd be a builder again.
> Everyone had to believe in 'some day,'
> except the ones who skirted the factory
> to walk down to the bay and then
> didn't stop. Rocks in their pockets.

The builder helped set up the frames
for the shacks, scrap wood scavenged
from who knows where, most of it
serving as a double wall. They all
had to make do, lucky the land
next to the boarded-up factory
was available. So many of them
knew too well their people's survival sagas.
> A mixed group, some singles,
> some families, folks recently
> arrived from Mexico, Russia,
> the Philippines, Ireland. Potato
> famine, pogroms, poverty.

They thought it wouldn't happen
again, not here in Gold Mountain.

"Sanctuary"
Millard Sheets, 1932

The Carousel and the War

Sailors and their girlfriends,
young men and their horses,
memories of pennants and races, spurs, spears.
Would they ride any other steed,
listen to aught but a red white 'n blue beat?
How many stories blended together
in order to enter the ride, clear the mind
of everything extraneous, no thought given
to longings for an afternoon of
lemonade and guitar picking,
or doubts about the stranger
riding on the next animal,
ally or enemy? Just for this ride,
this ten minutes, climb on the steed,
here's hurdy-gurdy music, up-down
all around past changing faces in
wavery mirrors and he stops wondering
what's waiting for him when he steps off
the revolving platform and leaves the ten minutes
of just-himself, the possible kiss,
the nonsensical tune.

"The Merry-Go-Round"
Charles Payzant, 1940

Down and Out

This man is not abstract, this man is not
old, not a boy, not too sick to work,
he could work, his hands and feet fine,
his hair is fine, he still has decent
shoes and coat and pants, yet he
sits dejected on the sidewalk curb. People
pass him by. Does he have a home to
go to? Is his mother still alive, where
will he sleep tonight? Does anyone
talk to him? This is not abstract,
how do I step out of my careful cocoon
and say to the down and out man
(alarm in the gut when I glimpse
his eyes go crazy), 'I wish I could
help, do you know where the soup
kitchen is, would a dollar do any good
at all?' Do I fear his 'bad luck' is
catching, do I fear that, if I take one step
into his reality, I won't make it back out?

"Forgotten Man"
Maynard Dixon, 1934

RESTLESS

Iris in the Sky

Someone who has the power to put
the iris in the sky. Snail looking up
from its post on the lower leaf. A certain
vantage point. Vulnerable body stretched
outside the shell, little antennae
guiding sight to the tender petal easily torn,
but there it is exposed to wind and
god knows what weather. Her hand is
near, delicate and clean and
unprotected. Certainly not a gardener,
yet the full-blown iris and its
companion bud look perfectly cared for.
As perfect as any flower can be. She
has it all under control: flower,
sky, hand, snail, leaves.
Yes, I say, I'd like a world like that.
Just please don't make me the snail.

"Poetic Justice"
Helen Lundenberg, 1942

Muse

Asking for beauty and getting the woman with
river hair and half a secret.
She could hold you down in a fight,
she could spell the letters in summer shapes.
Peach tree and paradise and broken night.
Do not doubt her blue-black archery.
She visits you in prison, she sends you spinning,
she shoves you out of the nest. She knows
how to fly. She unlocks the midnight door
for you, she forces you to sleep in the wild.
Riddles, historical evidence, and the same old thing.
Newly addressed, newly dressed, silver-haired
braids, stairs to climb. Cellar doors, a portable
stove, provisions enough for a week.
She never gives you a straight answer,
her alleyway's crooked and she doesn't live
there. Look for her in *evanesce*. She'll
meet you in *leave-breadcrumbs-for-the-birds*.

"The Muse"
Stanton MacDonald Wright, 1924

Cat and a Ball

Her cat sits, mornings, in the sun
on the window-seat, while she grumbles
out of bed, stumbles to the bathroom,
tells herself her dreams aren't real but
oh! she wishes to return to their ir-
reality, no matter how weird, because
look at the weirdness of the everyday
human world. Her cat purrs as she
runs fingertips over its fur, and how to
make it stronger, how to give it credit
and honor, really, for being such
a mainstay in her life? She wishes
she could have a chat with its feline
mind, wishes she knew how to purr
and be entranced by a red ball,
small but irresistible reason to live.

"Cat and a Ball on a Waterfall"
Ursula Barnes, 1948

The 1950s

When decks were called porches,
meadows were divided into rectangles, water
corralled, beds made square, colored blocks
one color or the other, and kids grew taller
than Father. She stands, back turned,
don't look at her face. So what if her feet are bare,
she doesn't stand in a meadow with bees or
other stings. The immigrant maid has wiped
and mopped the porch floor, it's clean.
Geometry contains. What's in the gift box?
No slithery tangled-up-nothing will escape,
the police-work is sorted, badges affixed.
She looks to the ocean, ever-moving,
uncontainable. Get it in the picture, use the opaque
blue, make a long straight line far away
across rectangular fields of monocrop.

"Figure on a Porch"
Richard Diebenkorn, 1959

Afraid of Mice

Not a man, this man. A force.
The Tibetan practice of Facing Our Fear
tells us, 'Picture it. Ask it what it
needs.' The force of fear. Everything
this body has endured, jamming up
the muscles, clogging the bloodstream,
x-ing out the ears, so shrill the keening.
A mouse, furry brown with red ears,
cracked body, a tail made of every
clown-face witnessed by the Fear.
Pauvre petite. Unstanchable
imagination, lion-head. What's it need?
It's big already, naked,
has no brain, nothing stands
between it and the needle-toothed,
what's-it-going-to-do creature
so near the not-man's foot.
Needs the clown-faces all to fall
in a heap, needs the lion to roar,
needs to invite the folks in the muscles
to start talking. Serve cocktails. Colors.
Get some clothes and a good sturdy pair
of shoes no needle-sharp teeth can puncture.
Get a friend who's not afraid of mice.

"The Mouse's Tail"
Jess (Collins), 1951–54

Slopes

This is how the day closes and thought gets lost.
The hills take over with their slopes, with their
harshness where the rocks break through, where
the trees are so tough a human can't find a way.
It's distance we want, the softening
of twilight, the invitation of night to lie
on the bed or in the stars, feel blood
making its map under the armories of skin.
Dreams are mind's unchosen path, chaos a gift,
nothing to finish or polish or push. Somewhere
on the planet, it's early spring and cherry blossoms
are breaking out of a black wood that
looks like death. A girl named Ann walks
in a muddy orchard where the late rain has
knocked a few white petals onto the mud at her
feet. She's in a state of love. No one needs
to answer her, no one needs to hold her hand,
she lives in the assurance of cherries.
The scent is wild, as new as any air ever gets.

"Mt. Holyoke #2"
Edward Corbett, 1960

April

The April artist. Mud ripens, rain loosens
to rivulets of chatter and squeak. Something beckons
from behind the barren trees. Monkey-face, butterfly-
scale. She opens the drapes, no longer as afraid as
she was last Saturday when everything was still so
white and the birds shy, even skittish. If she could,
what would she ask the April Fool? It wouldn't be
to grant a wish, Fool hasn't that particular power.
No, more something about how to see the defining
(or promissory) glint of water. Earthly water, sky water.
Or maybe how to be stupid enough to count on
roots. Or love. The flower fortune, 'loves-me, loves-
me-not.' Thinking about May (coming soon) and the May-
pole dance (makes one young again). She knows about
the rising up and the lying down. She smears her arms,
her face with the unhesitant light and no longer
has to think about whether it's worth it to live,
she just does.

"April 1957"
Frank Lobdell, 1957

Abstract

Where the opening provides the mood
to shift. Yes, pieces of black still — jazz
same as stripes on the yellow-jacket's
body. Some of us allergic,
a necessary counterpoint. Take
for example the cricket, and wait
for summer to favor fall.
The plum tree's leaves wrinkle slanted
morning, wrinkle brown into *upstanding*.
They'll drop in the pond, revise
the day's feel, but it isn't all black
or even gray though these are
the colors crickets display and their
ringing disharmony is jazz that
refers to dark. Little detectives
of cracks and crannies.
Openings favor escape. And so
it happens, the tightest structure
leaks. Though black swallows it,
color finds the scatter.
Nothing completely loses hope.

"Abstraction"
Sam Francis, 1959

Calendar

The twelve circles fit together all ways:
overlap, splash, radiate,
call to one another through opacity
that threatens to suffocate
unless.
The Sufis whirl.
Ballet master says, Choose a dot,
make your turn and back to
that dot
       each time
refocus
       the dot
and you won't get dizzy. The year
flares out
                flares — flares — flares
      until the light's distributed
      (remember the circle and the globe)
   then
contracts. The center's
dark pulls everything
   in until
unbearable heaviness begins
   again
      to spin. And spring. Spring.

"Ninnekah Calendar"
Lee Mullican, 1951

Mandala

Open. Open.
Close. Close.
Come close. Spread,
whirl, out the pen,
no more *when*, all *now*, no ow,
all nose, not refuse — not ref-use.
Fuse. Use all, no small
smell, well, round, bound, un-bound
bound-i-full, fall, down-wall
again. A gain. Again.

"Mandala"
Keith Sanzenbach, 1960

Sister Speaks to Brother

You don't remember where you left your family.
Now your fingerprints resemble
the woodpecker tracks we found in the dust
of the anthill under the desiccated oak's
trunk. What do you remember?
How to play detective with the mountain map,
the way you loved leftover snow patches
that traced the watercourses? Did you
follow the watercourses, did you find
your missing boots, how high did you
manage to climb? Oh, my brother,
can we multiply your absences until
they form some kind of pattern
we'll press to the emptiness you are?
Your banjo, the daisy crown you gave
your first girlfriend, your Levi's.
The way you swam without swim trunks.
Please come back before Mother dies.

"Shadow Repair for the Western Man"
William Allen, 1970

Dancer

An old man dances, having smoked a pipe,
having asked himself, 'Which animal helps
make me strong?' Sun took the whole
afternoon to slip downslope, shadows long.
It's his time of day. He's made it through
the morning which demanded that he
live and answer questions. Wraps himself
in leather, puts on his huge-eye mask and
hooves. Horns beside his ears, his old wife
made the strap that holds them on. Drum
in his hand, he's ready to talk with
the sun in this elder part of their day
together. Gather his legs under him,
gather his life around him. He was the boy
who ran the race and won, he was the man
for whom the animal gave its life. It's
the beast he dances. No longer tired, no longer
tangled in hope, he steps to his drum
in the dust until sun kisses the horizon.

"The Buffalo Dance"
Hassel Smith, 1960

Heritage

Charm. Pleasantly seductive.
Consider, for instance, the charm
bracelet. There's love there,
entertainment. There's totemic
power. 'Let me be like this butterfly,
ballerina, jaguar.' The most potent
meaning of 'charm' resides in its
synonym, 'spell.' The fairy godmother
cast a spell and the very nature
of a girl's life changed. The Toto Dancer
descends from the sky of the mind
and makes the mountains while
his giant caterpillar assistant
digs the riverbed out of the land.
Back and back and back through
inheritance and memory, we
conjure the gods who dance
Earth into being. What are the spells,
now, that would bind us to caring?

"Toto Dancer at Bloomer Hill"
Frank L. Day, 1973

Day of the Dead

When purposeful laughter mixes with departing spirits.
California dry riverbeds, spring-green hills turned
to toasted buns, summer having burned
all sweetness away and seeds given
DNA to carry, sleeping memory.
Parents try to get kids to parcel out
their Halloween candy and remember
that the costumes aren't supposed to be
all fun, but to carry the dark in a strong face
all the way into the absent, longed-for light.
And the grandparents, what do we tell them?
'Hang on, I know you don't walk so well but
we'll get you your flu shot, we'll light solstice
lights, we want you to pull through the waning.
Tell us your stories, sing us your songs, we are
here to show you it was worth the struggle, we'll
help you piece together your twists and turns,
the tortured steps you'd rather forget.'
Look at the brown and laden stems, twigs,
fallen branches. The rain will come, we'll sit
inside a warm house and watch it run down
the window pane. We'll be quiet.

"November 1964"
Alvin Light, 1964

Point of View

What he sees in his backyard, it's true, the bull
isn't there but he feels a cow-i-ness about the place
now that he's let the fescue grow. Cleared away
Himalayan berry bushes, thinking all along about
Brer Rabbit, now no more place to hide but he just
couldn't let those brambles lay claim to the only space
he could house a cow should he eventually wish to.
And the dogs are much happier this way even though
he's had to fence a patch for the daisies and
marigolds to grow, those mutts have no sense of
aesthetics though they do like going after the deer
and deer'll win the beauty contest every year.
'Course, a dog chases a deer for a completely other
purpose, let's not forget predation and the jugular.
Actually hasn't seen a deer nearby for months,
the fence around the garden's as much for deer
as for dogs, he knows soon's he accidentally
leaves the gate open, the ungulant telegraph'll
click into motion and, come morning, every one
of the party-dress petals will've disappeared down
a deer's gullet. They do seem to possess an aesthetic
sense but it's totally about appetite.

"Canine Point of View"
Roy De Forest, 1974

Party

That disfigured hawk hobbling in from the left,
he's a charmer, with the prayer shawl
draped over his right shoulder. A rarefied ocean wave
lifts his left wing toward the other party-people.
He isn't a threat, claws caught in cement.
If it weren't for the sharp beak, they'd all
cuddle up, a frenzy of petting, shared feathers
and stories: how mis-shapes can summon
alternate gestalts. It's an intuition of
attractions, a re-arrangement of sun's en-
couragement to worship. Tear apart formality,
dispense with blathering. That's what a day on
the beach is for — the liberating light,
the sudden ladders of color.

"Ocean Park Series"
John Altoon, 1962

Wave Sculpture

A thing like this starts small, a wave
in the ocean, a wave in the sculptor's studio.
Starts with a sigh so tentative it can't be
heard, no one knows it's begun, no one
can imagine its future size, or any ending,
or that it's important to get out of the way.
It's a natural thing in the ocean, belonging
to earth's heave and the huge body of water
it's part of. We do hear the sigh as it
grows audible, we watch as the water's
many sighs merge and move, creating a force
we know there's no stopping. Until the crash.
The shatter. As in the sculptor's hands, breath,
intent. Or, no intent, just a listening,
a touching, something rising inside her
to work itself out. Turn and twist and gleam,
grow taller, taller, more assertive than she'd
have thought, had she thought about it
before she began moving with the urge
she called the wave.

"Structure and Flow #2 (Wave)"
Claire Falkenstein, 1965

Brain Map

She wonders about the dark spots.
How they seem to connect to each other,
mysteriously, revealing nothing.
These lines like trails. Do they map the way
she learned? Events, practices she filed away
and forgot how to access them now?
And this part drifting like a cloudy white
answer, a beguilement she wants to get
close to. It all swirls, changes, drives toward
the center, only to sink into dark.
Where in her brain does memory lie?
Or is it not in one place? Scattered in these
broken directions, memories change, and
change again. She wants things to stay
the same, or at least that there be, in her
corridors and closets, a reliable source of
light. There is light, if she could direct it
to the wow! moments, gather some
of them together. The moment of her birth,
the smell of her mother's breasts, the first
word she understood, her first step.
Mother said she laughed, for the first time,
at the shadow-play on the tent roof.
Where, on her map, can she find
that laugh?

"At Last a Thousand II"
June Wayne, 1965

A Fish in Water

The orange fish rises to the surface
and the water, disturbed and challenged
in its course or its stillness,
changes what the human eye sees as fish.
A fracture of sunlight,
shattered path of flame, portrait
of rupturing ripple. How many ways can
one see a fish? There's the fish's
eye a black turning, a blindness,
marbled fortune-teller keeping
the truth to itself. What does one want
to know from a fish? How to be
beautiful and care nothing for it?
How to swim in a liquid we love
which would kill us? To be cold
to the bone, yet dance with
handsome, lissome Mr. Water,
live inside him, unmarried?

"Orange Fish"
Joseph Raffael, 1979

PRESERVE

Succession (1)

The bramble of barbed wire,
broken-down fence tangled over
an oak branch that forgot to stay
alive to see the way territorial markers
can break and let cows through.
This fence fumbled its duty.
Or was it the rancher who fled
for 'greener pastures' (concrete,
steel, and freedom from dung?).
Quite a contrast to turgid animal life,
always the hooves and hides
breaking through the ever-falling
fence, and the tramping into
poison-oak-infested underbrush
to get the cows back on open hills
where fast-drying grasses turn
a traitorous brown, and thistles
a cow can't eat invade pasture
flattened by hooves and hunger
and the human need for steak.

"Legacy" (I)
Paul Jossi, 1995

Succession (2)

Fences. Hold in. Keep out.
Stay close. Stay away. 'I own this,
you don't own this.' A tree
inside the fence learns about
barbs. Is this tree inside the
fence, or outside? Learning
about grow-here, don't-grow-there.
The fence breaks. The tree
reaches out and slowly rubs
against the wire, the post.
Wind pushes the branch hard
against the dead, used wood, a skreek
sounds again and again in the air,
no one comes to trim the branch
or rescue the abandoned fence.
They've gone. The livestock are gone.
Horsetail ferns spring up, rampant,
along the fence line. Rabbits come
and go, living trees' dead branches
stick around, cover for quail
and wood mice, dying leaves mulch
into soil where bracken spores
take root. Nothing against cows,
not to blame the humans who want
to own. They come and go.

"Legacy" (2)
Paul Jossi, 1995

Earthquake Country

The way the land shifts and rolls,
sometimes breaks, becomes a kind of evicting landlord
to roots that would rather stay put. Flimsy grip
on what is, after all, their parent.

Meantime, since we're in the here and now,
we appreciate the leftover cracks and crevices
where trapped water has saturated seeds sufficiently
a spree of grasses fluffs out, rinsing air
with what almost seems like the chatter of children
chasing the butterflies that frequent these
slopes and canyons — checkerspot, buckeye,
mourning cloak a brunette splotch in the blonde vista.

Sharp scent of sage startles flaccid nostrils,
breeze fiddles the live-oak leaves into a rusty
see-saw. What else is worth as much
as immersion in the water of now? The minutes
when earth stays steady underfoot and we
feel at home.

"Rancho Spring"
Jodi McKean, 2009

Sky

What do we want the sky
to be made of? The day-blue stretch
overhead we picture as
curved, a dome, a ceiling,
protective, yet we know
it expands forever. Where,
in its expanse, does it cease to be
blue, or white, pink, orange?
When does it lose the definition
we crave, the strength to protect
and allow us to dream?
Lie among the poppies, look
up. Either Everything is there or
clouds present us a playground
our minds can climb into, push
the whiteness this way and that
until a dragon forms. We want
to swing up and ride its back.

"Monte Bello, with Its Amazing Rolling Hills and Endless Blue Sky"
Oksana Baumert, 2010

Red

Within the storm cloud a red brain glows.
We realize we won't escape the universal mouth
with its unconscious teeth, free of malice, following
natural forms. The imbalance we've wrought
(following our instincts) earth's weather must
respond to. We dance within our ignorant web.
Our vaunted 'intelligence' can't save us though we
may conceive of reasons and remedies.
Our storm (red with awe, flooding with glory
for as long as we're able to see) has formed.
We are square in its path.

"California Storm Series #30"
Marvin Lipofsky, 1982–83

Berry Vine

The berry vine, forgotten by the namer of names.
But berry vines cannot be ignored.
They rule their plot of ground. Some
friendly, some full of briars, cruel.
Look beyond misery, consider the necessities
of survival, of bare and barren and bountiful.
Do the thorns prick other plants' flesh,
just as they do a human? And the plants
pull away, cede space or seep sap
onto the pricker that in some way feeds it?
Does human blood feed the berry vine's health?
We want Nature to be kind, call Her Mother,
we breathe green, wear sturdy boots
to tromp through detritus, deep into needles,
thorns, the threat of bears, to penetrate
to the hoary, silent, grand old mothers.
Place our palms on the moss and crevasses
of bark, pray to a being that has made it this far.

"Full Fog"
Bob Clark, 2010

Autumnal Equinox

A morning that bends into itself, black
branch bereft of leaves, season
when losing is the lesson. Listen
for signals in the somnolent air. Fog
siphoned through with orange and rust.
Birds hanging on by claw and wish. Look
at this one with his bright red head
defying gray air, the downward bent.
Can't stay sun's southward journey
but sing a little in the see-saw of season,
equinox an equation of forces.
Place recumbency one side, place
thrust the other. Don't you see them
raise a red feather, drop a dark
blue in the duff where bare-branched
memory is tucked?

"Colorful Gray Day"
Elyse Dunnahoo, 2010

Fog

Feathery fog inches its sly way
over the humps and into the crevices
of the land. It's evening and the sun
has been a bully since eleven a.m.,
pushing last night's fog down
to progenitor ocean where it rests
and waits. It's a traveler, a wooer,
it whispers over the heated grasses,
places a wet word on recumbent
leaves, the needles of evergreens,
mosses that lift tiny digits
to wick into hidden roots.
Who can see through fog? The meadows
and forests go blind, creatures —
owl, raccoon, deer — must feel
their way in their night hunts. Toads,
frogs, salamanders, bask in the damp
bath, and rocks far up on the beach
once again feel ocean's kiss.

"Kings Mountain Evening"
Rebecca Holland, 2010

Sequoia

The giant sequoia stills all doubt.
The older these trees get, the likelier
they'll live forever. Huge peace.
A host on a radio show interviewed a man
who'd spent decades exploring the heights
of old-growth redwoods. Awestruck.
A devotee. The interviewer confessed she'd never
seen an old-growth redwood. Through the radio
came a shocked, dumbstruck pause.
Then the man said, as though it were impossible,
'You've never gone to see the redwoods?'
Her voice revealed the embarrassment that
must have burned on her face. 'I guess I need
to do that.' She lived in California.
These trees answer your prayers.

"The Grizzly Giant Sequoia, Mariposa Grove, California"
Albert Bierstadt, 1872

September

Right there on the whorl, the colors
utter a riposte to wind's lachrymal
wooing. Plenty of people pass by
without even hearing the ongoing
talk.

      Where leaves percolate
deer crackle and malingerer lizard
dreams an enduring lecture
that explains the nature of the sun
on sixteen different days. He's so
tired, yet there are these requirements
of worship

      again and again.
The time comes when branches
droop, begin to doubt the truth
of sun at all, that's when lizard
has retired into the phantasmagoria
of cold despair

      and cannot help.
But still there's sound. Skunk
wears the robe of night,
raccoon wears the mask,
they rub against the trees
in passing, that's when a great sigh
penetrates even the stone
lizard sleeps under.

"September Song"
Paul Jossi, date unknown

Acknowledgments for LENS

"The Muse" and "Sister Speaks to Brother" (formerly titled: "Shadow Repair for the Western Man") published in *The California Quarterly*, vol. 39, #3.

"September" published in *poetrymagazine.com*, Anthologies Fall issue, 2014.

"Near Lone Pine" published in *West Trestle Review* Spring 2015; republished in *Lilipoh* Fall 2015; republished in *Canary* Summer 2016.

"Easter Harvest" and "Canyon, Santa Barbara" published in *The California Quarterly*, vol. 40, #3.

"Abstract" published in *Ambush Review # 5*, 2016.

"The Artist Paints Light," "Coming Into," and "Cat and a Ball" published in *Ekphrastic California*, Winter 2016.

"Oranges" published in *Green Hills Literary Lantern*, XXVII (2016), republished in *Lilipoh* Winter 2017.

"Thirst" published in *Third Wednesday*, Fall/Winter 2016/2017.

"Autumnal Equinox" and "Sky" published in *The Peacock Journal*, January 2018.

"Slopes" published in *Miramar* 7, under title: "To Edward Corbett's Mt. Holyoke #2," 2018.

"Canyon, Santa Barbara," "Earthquake Country," and "Succession (2)" published in the anthology, *Fire and Rain, Ecopoetry of California*, 2018.

About the Author

Grace Marie Grafton is the author of six books of poetry. *Jester* (2013) was published by Hip Pocket Press. Author Mary Mackey writes that this collection of poems "links us to a communal imagination which transcends the conventional limits of both poetry and fine arts." *Whimsy, Reticence and Laud* (2012) was published by Poetic Matrix Press. Poet/novelist Tobey Hiller writes of this book, "In these lush sonnets...the wild and the cultivated often collide." *Other Clues* (2010), composed of experimental prose poems, was published by Latitude Press. Of this collection, poet Melissa Kwasny writes, "There is wisdom amidst the chaos. Eros. Nature. There are tutelary spirits of the plants and the nouns." Ms. Grafton's chapbook *Zero* (1999) won the Poetic Matrix Press contest. Her poetry has won honors from "Bellingham Review," San Francisco PEN Women's Soul Making contests, "Sycamore Review" and "Anderbo." Her poems have recently appeared in "Fifth Wednesday," "Cortland Review," "Ambush Review," "Askew," "The Offending Adam," "Sin Fronteras," and others.

For over three decades, Ms. Grafton taught children to write poetry through the CA Poets in the Schools program, winning twelve Artist in Residence grants from the CA Arts Council for her teaching. She was awarded Teacher of the Year by the River of Words Youth Poetry Contest, sponsored by Robert Hass, US Poet Laureate.

About the Press

Unsolicited Press is a small press in Portland, Oregon. The small press is fueled by voracious editors, all of whom are volunteers. The press began in 2012 and continues to produce stellar poetry, fiction, and creative nonfiction.

Learn more at www.unsolicitedpress.com.

CPSIA information can be obtained
at www.ICGtesting.com
Printed in the USA
FSHW010533300919
62511FS